Faith Matters

The Breakthrough You Want

www.FaithMattersToYou.com

Glen Aubrey

Creative Team Publishing
Fort Worth, Texas

© 2019 by Glen Aubrey.

All rights reserved. No part of this book may be reproduced, stored in a retrieval system or transmitted in any form or by any means without the prior written permission of the publisher, except by a reviewer who may quote brief passages in a review distributed through electronic media, or printed in a newspaper, magazine, or journal.

Disclaimers:

- Due diligence has been exercised to obtain written permission for use of references, quotes, or imagery where required. Any additional quotes, references, or imagery may be subject to the Fair Use Doctrine. Where additional references, quotes, or imagery may require source credit, upon written certification that such a claim is accurate, credit for use will be noted on www.FaithMattersToYou.com.
- The opinions and conclusions expressed are solely those of the author and/or the individuals and entities represented and are limited to the facts, experiences, and circumstances involved. No professional, psychological, or medical advice is implied, stated, or offered in any way whatsoever. You are encouraged to seek professional help, education, advice, and counsel from individuals you deem competent should you desire to learn more about Christian spirituality, human behavior, self-confidence, or any related topic.
- Note that certain names and related circumstances may have been changed to protect confidentiality. All stories where names are mentioned are used with the permission of the parties involved, if applicable. Any resemblance to past or current people, places, circumstances, or events is purely coincidental.

Website: Randy Beck www.mydomaintools.com
Cover design: Justin Aubrey

ISBN: 978-0-9979519-7-4

PUBLISHED BY CREATIVE TEAM PUBLISHING
www.CreativeTeamPublishing.com
Ft. Worth, Texas
Printed in the United States of America

Faith Matters

The Breakthrough You Want

Glen Aubrey

*****

Hebrews 11:1, King James Version (KJV):

"Now faith is the substance of things hoped for, the evidence of things not seen."

*****

Hebrews 11:1, New International Version (NIV):
"Now faith is confidence in what we hope for and assurance about what we do not see."

*****

Contents

Hebrews 11:1, King James Version (KJV) and New International Version (NIV)	5
Dedication	
A Legacy of Faith	11
Endorsements	13
This Book	21
The Strongest Foundation	
If God Be For Us, Who Can Be Against Us?	35
Light of Love, music group, 1974, photo	35
If God Be for Us, lyrics, music	38
Chapter 1	
What Matters to You, Matters Most	47
Chapter 2	
The Desire for a Breakthrough	55
The Core Team: A Functioning Workable Solution (Table)	56
Values, Vision, Mission, and Message	57
The Four Questions	58

Contents

Chapter 3
    Authentic Faith in Action   69

Chapter 4
    Undeniable Facts   75
    His Love for Us, lyrics   80

Chapter 5
    As an Example   83
    As an Example, music score, lyrics   84

Chapter 6
    The Practice of Faith   89
        Authentic Faith Touches Other People in Need through Us   96

Chapter 7
    Some Things Matter, Some Things Don't   99

Chapter 8
    Break Through!   107

Chapter 9
    Share Your Journey   113
        Emmy® 2011   117

Chapter 10
    Be Thankful as You Accept God's Grace and Proclaim His Truth   121

Contents

Closing Thoughts	*131*
There Is a Redeemer, lyrics and music	*133*

*****

Recommended Reading	*135*
Credits in Order of Appearance	*137*
Products and Services	*141*
The Author	*143*
The Publisher	*145*

*****

Dedication
A Legacy of Faith

My wife, Cindy, and I were both raised in families where authentic faith and trust in God were practiced. This was the example set by our parents. At early ages, long before she and I ever knew each other, we chose to become believers.

Cindy and I passed along our faith to our children. Our daughter, Heather, and our son, Justin, followed in our footsteps.

Now our children's children are being raised in homes of authentic faith. Heather and her husband have given us five grandsons and Justin and his wife have given us three granddaughters. All of them are "faith people" and we are thrilled that they are daily practicing what they have chosen to believe.

I dedicate this book to my family, in celebration of *A Legacy of Faith.*

~ Glen Aubrey, August, 2019

Endorsements

Bruce Broadfoot
Mortgage Loan Officer
First Tenor, *Light of Love*

If you seek a life of fulfillment, read **Faith Matters**. If you're wondering what makes an excellent leader, read **Faith Matters**.

My favorite passage: "*I define a 'relationship' as the choice I make about other people's success, changing my behavior to help them win.*"

When the success you long for eludes, seek Him, because **Faith Matters**. When God blesses you immeasurably, be grateful, because **Faith Matters**. When you're on a roll, be humble, because **Faith Matters**. When grief overwhelms you, keep believing, because **Faith Matters.**

Glen helps the reader examine what is most critical to each of us, and why. He leads us to experience an authentic breakthrough so our lives are richer in countless ways.

Thanks, Glen!

*****

Endorsements

Deborah Little, Friend of Author
Retired Director of Assisted Living
Mount Miguel Covenant Village, Spring Valley, California

Faith is at the very heart of our relationship with God. He created us to be in relationship with Him. If you feel like your relationship is not all it could or should be, perhaps it is a matter of faith. Maybe you need a breakthrough.

We are all at different places in our walk with the Lord, as each person's journey is personal and unique. This book may serve as a tool to help you dig into your own faith, and see what may be missing, or at least underdeveloped.

I feel very blessed to have grown up with a very childlike faith that was nurtured in every aspect of my life. Not all have had that privilege, but that need not hold you back.

What matters now is that you explore the elements that are present in authentic faith. Why not start here, with *Faith Matters*?

*****

Monica Hunter, Friend of Author

Faith Matters is biblically based with insightful nuggets and truths! These things brought smiles to my face and made my heart sing! The book reveals obvious applications of truth.

Glen, you are a gifted musician, lyricist, and poet and you have an affinity for melodic sentences.

I endorse *you* as your friend.

*****

Endorsements

John E. Christiansen
CPT, U.S. Army (pilot, Vietnam), Technical Sales Engineer, Educator (technical theater, chemistry), church lay leader.

While I am an avid reader, I am more likely to be reading history or mystery than a "religious" book. I found *Faith Matters* to be a most enjoyable read.

Glen provides several fundamentals of Christian life with the emphasis that the faith that matters is a lifelong process, not just a "mountaintop" experience. I would recommend it to anyone who is seeking a deeper relationship with Christ.

*****

Deanna Harrington Christiansen, Poet

This small, easily read volume happily reminds me of the old hymn, "Tell Me the Old, Old Story (of Jesus and His love)". What *Faith Matters* presents is not unheard of—except by some.

For you who are searching for a breakthrough—or even a fullness of faith—it will figure among those foundational things that will make all the difference in you. The Story is indeed of God's unmovable love for you, and God's abiding invitation to you to "Come and see".

Some of this old hymn's lyrics plead
"Tell me the story often,
 For I forget so soon."
You will return often to what are "indisputable facts" from Scripture, as Glen assures us in *Faith Matters*, as your life in Christ matures: that's where the Old, Old Story of

Endorsements

Christ's love for you will manifest itself as ever-new, ever-wondrous, ever-needed, and always just what the soul hungers for.

You will find that maturing into the person God created you to be contrasts to merely human maturing, which is toward independence from parents; rather, it will see you growing ever more Godward, dependent upon—not independent of—God; and blessedly so.

In his "Closing Thoughts", Glen Aubrey summarizes clearly, "…the Breakthrough in relation with God is the transformation of our entire way of living, our entire selves, by Him." *Faith Matters* will encourage you in that.

> ~ "Tell Me the Old, Old Story" is in the Public Domain. Poem by English Evangelist Katherine Hankey, 1866. Music by Rt. Rev. George Washington Doane.

*****

Mike Atkinson
Publisher of *MIKEY'S FUNNIES*
www.mikeysFunnies.com
A clean humor email list with over 25,000 subscribers

I've known Glen Aubrey for many years. We've had many dealings together. His books are intriguing and inspiring.

Faith Matters explores the essence of a key element of the Christian experience. And that's the point.

Enjoy this book with me.

*****

Endorsements

Nate Grella, Pastor
Compass Christian Church, North Fort Worth, Texas

"Just have faith." Maybe someone has said those words to you, and you've questioned whether or not that is possible. Maybe someone has said that about your relationship with God.

"Just have faith." What does this kind of faith look like? How do we know that we've attained it? I think these are questions many people wrestle with or may not know the answer to.

That's what I love about this book. Glen makes it easy for us to not only understand what authentic faith should look like, but how we live it out in our lives. As I read through the pages of this book, it felt like I was having a conversation, much like many of those Glen and I have had during the time we've know each other.

His words are authentic and wise, and help those who are on the journey to understand just how important our faith is, as believers.

My prayer is that this book would help you find the breakthrough you need when it comes to your faith.

*****

Tim Woolpert, Singer, Songwriter

As a child, I was force-fed religion. I was told what to believe and when to believe it. This would ultimately cause me to rebel. A wise man once told me later in life, "A church

Endorsements

is just a place where people meet to share in their faith, and that anywhere I laid my head down to pray could be my church." I have always battled with my faith but have always maintained a level of faith that sees me through and comforts me when I seek salvation.

As Glen wrote, "Even for those who may profess to not believe, or have little or no faith in God, their daily experiences with faith prove consistency in belief and practice of some kind of faith to varying degrees."

This book has given me so much insight into a man I consider to be a dear friend, insight into a man with unbreakable faith, and insight into who I am, and who I wish to be. Faith matters very much and finding it completely will be my ultimate journey.

Glen, I thank you for giving me the inspiration to rediscover not only who I am, but why I am.

*****

Vernon Lintvedt, Pastor
Blessed Savior Lutheran Church, O'Fallon, Illinois
Baritone, *Light of Love*

Faith Matters is a personal journal/manual describing and illustrating the essential components of faith revealed through biblical quotations, and supported by a sampling of original musical compositions, personal stories, original poetry, and writings.

Faith Matters is also a motivational book in which Glen Aubrey weaves personal reflections with Scripture, inviting the reader into the realm of authentic faith.

Endorsements

He expresses the hope that the mature in faith will grow stronger and more confident in their faith-walk with Christ, and that the spiritually ambivalent, having little or no faith, may be drawn into the power of a living and dynamic faith, so that when they come to the conclusion of the book they might read the clever title with a slightly different punch of emphasis: "Faith Matters!"

Give it a read!

*****

This Book

I want to tell you a true story.

It was early January of 2019. A dear friend sent me a text in which she wished us both a Breakthrough for the New Year. In gratitude for her kindness, I asked her what she meant. Well, it was for both of us to discover what the meaning was.

While we are both "faith people" and have deep roots and a history of belief and trust in God, we were at a loss to know for certain what a Breakthrough for each of us was or could be. Could it be financial success, personal victories in the future for us yet to experience, or spiritual renewal? Could this Breakthrough encompass maybe all three and even more?

Over time, several months in fact, the truth of a Breakthrough definition became much clearer. Without any hesitation I'll share it with you now.

One of my first thoughts was to revisit the Fruit of the Spirit passage in the Book of Galatians, specifically **Galatians 5:22 and 23, New International Version (NIV)**:

22 But the fruit of the Spirit is love, joy, peace, forbearance, kindness, goodness, faithfulness, 23 gentleness and self-control. Against such things there is no law.

I pondered and prayed, but that list, though powerful, wasn't totally "it," although what "it" finally became certainly included the elements of that scripture.

The Breakthrough encompasses all that we desire and need according to God's perfect will when we explore and live in what faith in God and His principles and practices really mean. It is His true, verifiable, life-changing, and authentic faith.

> The Breakthrough encompasses all that we desire and need according to God's perfect will when we explore and live in what faith in God and
> His principles and practices really mean.
> It is His true, verifiable, life-changing, and authentic faith.

The Breakthrough is not a wish or a dream coming true, although wishing, and dreaming, and even working for the dream are actions in which we all engage from time to time.

It's much more.

Faith Matters

How many times have you dwelt on an idea, considered it then actually tried to implement plans to little avail or resulting in abject failure?

One thing I have learned: God is not the author of confusion, missteps, or mistakes. His guidance is always right, His timing always perfect.

> God is not the author of confusion, missteps, or mistakes. His guidance is always right, His timing always perfect.

Trust and experience teach us how faith should work and how we live and express ourselves as people of faith, even though our interpretation is and must always be subject to His desires for us.

Frankly I've known and experienced God's assurance for a long time, yet I still at times, even often, choose and move unadvisedly, too quickly, or without sufficient waiting on Him. Perhaps you have done this, too. When we do, we are amazed at how "un-peaceful" life seems to be.

I attended my sophomore and junior years of college in Pasadena, California, two hours from my original home which was located in San Diego. Financially, I was "a starving college student" who was barely able to make ends meet even though I had a job and a scholarship.

One day without any warning or foreknowledge, an envelope with handwriting I did not recognize, almost like a right handed person addressed it with a left hand, was delivered to my mailbox at my apartment in Pasadena. In it was a twenty dollar bill. No note was included, nothing more that would indicate where it had come from, or from whom. To this day, although I have a hunch of the source, I still don't know for sure. It had not come from my parents or any other relative ... I checked. I knew then of no one who was the giver.

Interestingly, the same amount in the same kind of envelope came at the first of the month for every month I lived in Pasadena, without fail. It always came on time ... never early or late.

I remember thinking then that God's timing is always perfect, meeting a need through someone's generosity, even though through whom I was clueless. In the economy of that day, it was a fair amount of money, certainly helping in times of deep need.

Perfect timing occurred again a few months later when I chose to depart my current employment to seek a similar position in Covina, about thirty miles distant. A letter offering me the position arrived on the day I had to make my choice, not a moment too soon and not one day late. I remember being amazed at the timing of God's provision.

Faith Matters

Clearly I've never forgotten the facts of these events including the truth of receiving without even asking and a job that just "fit" in time and place. Other times in life I have asked, but no fulfillment of any requests ever hit me harder in a good way, than receiving that monetary provision regularly from an anonymous donor and being offered a much better employment in a town close to the college for my fourth year, located in Azusa.

I accepted both gratefully, realizing authentic faith was at work, although I did not know how to express it fully then.

Faith matters. So does the absence of faith. This book is designed to exercise and celebrate authentic faith, and to encourage willful participation from all people who seek to know God more.

"Authentic faith" is a key phrase I ask us to consider, because I'm convinced that not all activity or passions that often accompany faith, or faith systems, are the real deal. What I am writing about isn't emotionally conceived or driven, though emotions often accompany true and authentic faith when we engage in it.

> This book is designed to exercise and celebrate authentic faith, and to encourage willful participation from all people who seek to know God more.

This faith is highly personal and to be shared, all at the same time. So a Breakthrough for me is, or should be, an encouragement to you and others, a promise in which we can participate, because no one has a corner on this faith ... it's available to all.

Faith Matters is the title of the book, of course. The word 'matters' is both a noun and a verb, depending on your intent of use. I mean it both ways.

The faith I'm talking about is part of godly character, not contrived or manufactured. A nugget is this: if we want more faith, we must identify what makes faith as believers in Christ and Christ-followers truly authentic and worth the individual life change that must accompany it. Real life change for the better is necessary when authentic faith is desired and present.

> Real life change for the better is necessary when authentic faith is desired and present.

What makes faith and hope authentic? I believe authenticity rests upon verifiable and unchanging truth. We can and should possess confident assurance in faith and hope because of the evidence. We can express confidence because we know and believe unchangeable and verifiable truth.

Faith Matters

Pure and precious hope is directly tied to authentic faith. Hope lives when faith is active.

> Hope lives when faith is active.

> We can and should possess confident assurance in faith and hope because of the evidence.

In 2009 I wrote the book, *Freedom Light, Expressions of Hope and Evidence,* **ISBN 9780979735875**. It developed into a deep and moving work of poetry, encouraging and relevant.

Freedom Light is based on **Hebrews 11:1**. Quoting from the **King James Version (KJV)**:

"Now faith is the substance of things hoped for, the evidence of things not seen."

In the Preface to *Freedom Light,* I quoted from *Core Teams Work*. Reflecting the newest version here, © 2019, page 13:

"Confidence is composed of two core elements. One is *hope*. Hope is a wish or a dream, but it is also more. Here it constitutes a strong and continuing desire for the good, right, and true. Hope that does not disappoint, and is not disappointed, focuses and frames best results that may come to pass if enough diligent effort is put forth.

"The second element is *evidence*. This is proof of a result that is sure to come. When right motives and dedicated actions are combined toward fulfillment of a worthwhile endeavor, evidence states that winning [fulfilled results] will occur. Completion of a goal may reside in the future, but the indication of good outcome is based on confirmed and irrefutable testimony. History proves that enduring and positive results come to pass when correct belief and right action are purposefully aligned and combined.

"Confidence interweaves hope and evidence. Assurance of outcomes requires more than wishful thinking—it demands repeatable proofs based on past demonstrations that truth wins. It always has; it forever will."

Authentic faith and the hope that accompanies it are not based just on theory or a wish upon a star. Authentic faith is anchored on facts. These represent the source of our confidence.

Author E. Stanley Jones wrote a book that changed my life. I bought it in 1973. It is titled **The Word Became Flesh**. I have studied this volume and treasure it to this day.

It impacted me so much (and still does) that I purchased several copies, one of which I gave to my son, Justin, in 2018. He and I have studied it daily, and have met monthly to go over pertinent passages.

E. Stanley Jones was a missionary, minister, philosopher and adventurer. He was born January 3, 1884, at Baltimore, MD and died January 25, 1973, in Bareilly, India.

The Word Became Flesh centers on the Word of God revealed in the life and person of Jesus Christ, becoming flesh extended in those who follow Him.

Three essential and indisputable facts make the Word becomes flesh become flesh again in us and our system of belief and practice. These facts are Jesus' birth, death, and resurrection.

The central verse, around which the entire book by E. Stanley Jones is composed, is **John 1:14**, from the **King James Version (KJV)**:

> And the Word was made flesh, and dwelt among us, (and we beheld his glory, the glory as of the only begotten of the Father,) full of grace and truth.

Grace frames the truth. This is important. We know that truth can be spoken without grace, and perhaps you and I have had to receive truth alone. When truth is proclaimed without grace, it can be hard to hear and is devoid of the one characteristic that demonstrates God's love in action, though not deserved.

That characteristic is grace, unmerited favor, freely offered to all. Though we are not worthy, God offers grace anyway. It can't be bought or sold ... it is a gift. And we have to willingly receive the gift to recognize and respond to God's truth through faith. Look at this well-known and often quoted verse:

Ephesians 2:8-9 (NIV):

[8] For it is by grace you have been saved, through faith—and this is not from yourselves, it is the gift of God— [9] not by works, so that no one can boast.

Only when we believe the facts, receive His grace, and embody Christ through His Holy Spirit can we understand and experience authentic, life-changing faith and all that accompanies it. It affects us because it must when we are willing to choose a faith life.

Our faith becomes authentic when we embody those truths not just as history but as living reality today. Our reality expands to include our second birth (being born again) or salvation, our dying to self which is willfully putting His will before ours, and our ultimate destiny, one uniquely tied to His resurrection life.

Faith Matters

Our outcomes include breaking through barriers that hinder authentic faith. The barriers can be many.

But we can be confident in God's provision. It is strong and enduring. God never fails.

When personal desires cooperate with, and do not counteract His will, we can experience God's peace, regardless of circumstances. Authentic faith and our obedience compose our Breakthrough. In this faith we possess eternal hope in Christ.

> A Breakthrough of faith is composed of two elements. One is deep personal desire and the other is God's will and our full submission to it.

This Breakthrough is evidenced in our daily activity. We become reflections of what we believe and practice. Desires and motives combine.

> Authentic faith and our obedience compose our Breakthrough. In this faith we possess eternal hope in Christ.

As a matter of course, we reflect our core, what makes us to be the real us, as examples of what really matters personally and what we consider important. When authentic faith truly matters, we showcase true faithfulness. When authentic faith doesn't matter, or is substituted by something far less, unbelief and confusion tend to take over. Then we often wallow in uncertainty, wander and project doubt and unstable opinion, or willfully choose a downright refusal of truth.

Observe the stark contrasts between meaningless talk and vibrant faith. Let's reference **I Timothy 1:3-7 (NIV)** where the Apostle Paul wrote to his student and mentee, Timothy:

> [3] As I urged you when I went into Macedonia, stay there in Ephesus so that you may command certain people not to teach false doctrines any longer [4] or to devote themselves to myths and endless genealogies. Such things promote controversial speculations rather than advancing God's work—which is by faith. [5] The goal of this command is love, which comes from a pure heart and a good conscience and a sincere faith. [6] Some have departed from these and have turned to meaningless talk. [7] They want to be teachers of the law, but they do not know what they are talking about or what they so confidently affirm.

On one side is mere conversation, including false teaching and endless debate, while on the other is conversion and willful obedience, including behavioral changes that bring life, a purposeful, personal, and exemplary one, illustrating and following God's will as a vibrant testimony to truth and our agreement with it.

We are given instructions in scripture pertaining to God's will, what spiritual conditions are most favorable for discovering it and following it. Discovering His will and "approving" it are possible with a renewed mind, one rebirthed and centered on God, in contrast to following ambitions apart from Godly influence. The writer of Romans put it this way in **Romans 12:2 (NIV)**:

> Do not conform to the pattern of this world, but be transformed by the renewing of your mind. Then you will be able to test and approve what God's will is — his good, pleasing and perfect will.

How many times have you witnessed or even been part of meaningless talk that ultimately does no one, or very few, any good? Obviously the injunction here is to avoid it, and that is wise advice. Replace it with willing obedience to Christ and what He wants for you. Ask Him to renew your mind (the ways you receive information, think, and process) so that your concentration is on His words and His way.

We learn that faith, hope, and love are part of the same package. According to **I Corinthians 13:13**, love is the "greatest of these."

Faith matters and hope is born. Love is the motive behind all of it. The reason you and I can dwell in, and practice authentic faith, is because God honors our faith because He loves us.

His Love endures through all time and is available to everyone. All we need to do to realize the Breakthrough of faith is to accept God's love and give Him control. We choose to follow and obey Him.

This choice is the best one.

> All we need to do to realize the Breakthrough of faith is to accept God's love and give Him control.
> We choose to follow and obey Him.

The Strongest Foundation

If God Be For Us, Who Can Be Against Us?

Romans 8:31b (KJV):
If God be for us, who can be against us?

The process of learning authentic faith was begun early. While a college-age student, I wrote this song. The era was the 70s and it was a time of spiritual growth, maturity, and application, especially in music for me.

If God Be for Us
Recorded by *Light of Love*, 1974

If God be for us,
Who can be against us?
For there's nothin' (ah), nothin' at all (Oh no),
That is stronger than His love (Oh, listen now),

He is our strength each passing day
And He will never let us fall (no, no),
And when trials come to block the way,
He is stronger than them all.

Light of Love, 1974, SW 1050 Studio West LCCN 95785910, © 1974 by Glen Aubrey, © 2019 by Glen Aubrey. All Rights Reserved.

Abraham Lincoln was once asked if God was on the side of the Union. His reply was insightful:

> "Sir, my concern is not whether God is on our side; my greatest concern is to be on God's side, for God is always right."

> How does one know he or she is on God's side?
> By willingly giving Him control and
> living in authentic faith.

There is no stronger foundation on which to build a life than God's unwavering commitment to your wellbeing and care.

Light of Love was a unique and inspiring musical group. Formed in 1974, it presented contemporary musical programs to thousands in Southern California.

On the next page is a photo of the group taken at Skyline Wesleyan Church, Lemon Grove, California in 1974.

The song's verses come next, followed by a scan of the original *Light of Love* arrangement of *If God Be for Us*.

Faith Matters

Light of Love

From left to right: Glen Aubrey, arranger, pianist;
Bruce Broadfoot, first tenor; Vernon Lintvedt, baritone;
Randy Smith, lead.

Glen Aubrey

Verses for *If God Be for Us* recorded on the *Light of Love* album:

(1) If you're strugglin' by yourself
To get the devil off of your back (Get him off!),
There's a way to set him runnin' so fast
And repel his worst attack.
Just put your trust in God alone,
He will fight the war for you.
And when you're sold out to God completely,
Well, winnin' is all you can do!

(2) If the plans that you have carefully made
Are just not turnin' out like they should (Not at all!),
Don't you know if you're a child of God,
They will all work out for good.
Just put your trust in the love of God
For His love will always endure.
And if you see there's a trial to overcome,
Well, love will do it for sure!

*****

Faith Matters

Glen Aubrey

Faith Matters

Chapter 1
What Matters to You, Matters Most

Even for those who may profess to not believe, or have little or no faith in God, their daily experiences with faith prove consistency in belief and practice of some kind of faith to varying degrees.

Take the chair in which you sit. Do you personally know the manufacturer or chair designer? Yet without that knowledge you may sit in the chair with full confidence that the chair will do for you what you want: support you without breaking apart.

Of course, there are exceptions ... in fact, over the years I have sat in a few chairs that have crumbled and nearly took me with them. This didn't happen too often, thankfully; but I remember.

Fully convinced and believing or not, we all choose levels of faith constantly. These choices, large or small, are a part of everyday living.

In what or whom do we trust and place faith, trust, and confidence? How do life's experiences shape us and what we believe truth to be, and how much do we rely on our wealth of life experiences, teachings, observations, and quests for knowledge and truth?

> Fully convinced and believing or not, we all choose levels of faith constantly. These choices, large or small, are a part of everyday living.

From the opening of *Freedom Light*:

"Your quests for enduring, principled truth and life application should include acquiring information from proven instructors whom you respect but must not be limited exclusively to their proclamations or interpretations. Apart from personal exploration — your own discovery, struggle, and conclusions — your journey is not complete."

Our understandings of truth and what really matters as a result of truth, upon which we choose to rely, require dedication and heightened degrees of sincerity, constantly discovering, learning, growing, and weighing what we learn and encounter. We can be sincerely right or sincerely wrong depending on what we choose and accept as truth and whether or not it is verifiable and consistent over time.

Faith Matters

From the *Freedom Light* Dedication:

"Sincerity is a choice of positive attitude and devotion at profound depths of reason, spirit, and emotion. It is a trait shared by balanced and maturing people, those not content with cursory, unproven, ritualistic simplicities. Sincerity pierces walls of insecurity, dissuades dogmatic inhibitions, and reveals and removes unnerving distractions. You are exercising sincerity when you engage fully in quests to enrich your life and the lives of others.

"***Freedom Light*** is dedicated to people of sincerity. If you are a searcher unsatisfied with anything other than continuing processes of dedicated discovery, accept that you are numbered with a few consecrated souls. These people of integrity and inward determination recognize that one of God's greatest gifts is desire, the insatiable longing for knowledge, faith, maturity, activity, and enduring right relationships.

"If you, like me, are one who yearns for more, read on. This work is for us."

From the book's Preface:

"A venture apart from enlightenment and encouragement can be immeasurably long and ultimately unfulfilled, certainly unfruitful. This book encourages you to live in confidence, and to experience internal satisfaction, assured of outcomes because you live in truth.

"*Freedom Light* explores release from distraction, and provides motivation to creatively act and respond. Life lessons born of truth and borne on duplicative examples are validated through the ages beyond time. They reside in principles and verifiable actions where positive results flourish and from which great stories are composed and told.

"This book celebrates their composition and contributions to a person's wellbeing … Your quests are important. Impacted by needs of the moment while anchored to ideals of the past, integrity-driven investigations live within the frameworks of eternally abiding truth.

"Your perspectives differ from those of others. Bring yours with you, employ them, never cease to ask questions, try to define what you discover, and wonder at what you cannot see materially.

"Your life will be richer for the adventure as will the experiences of those who, like you, search steadily for ultimate realizations, many of which may not be fulfilled in this life. Seek them regardless.

Faith Matters

"As you read, appreciate your options, your golden opportunities. Enjoy every minute of discovery. Every one counts for more than anyone could possibly envision."

Does your life matter? Absolutely. Do your quests for truth and faith matter? Resoundingly, "Yes!" Does what you believe come with consequences? Most assuredly.

It is vital for you and me to fully appreciate that we are created with insatiable desires to know more, learn, and grow. Stifling these desires is nothing short of tragic and misguided. Those desires are God-birthed and God-ordained.

We venture forth, discovering opportunities to learn all we can and then rely on what is proven worthy of our consideration. We choose our beliefs based on what we accept as truth, and then we produce actions based on those beliefs.

What you and I believe, and why, is vital to living at peace with ourselves and in confidence. The quest for faith in what we choose to believe is constant; it never ceases.

But what if our choices of belief are proven to be wrong or are shown to be based on data that under closer examination is proven not to be true at all?

That is an experience for many.

Maybe you are one of those who are not satisfied with what you have learned and discovered so far, and desire a realm of truth that rings more true.

If so, then welcome to the wide expanse of God-inspired wisdom and discernment. You and your investigation and discovery are welcomed.

At some point in our processes of discovery and investigation, we come to realize this: limits exist. There are many truths we may not learn in this life. There are causes of experiences in ourselves and others that we cannot explain.

We see lawlessness go unpunished, or become accepted, and wonder why. Injustice flourishes alongside justice, even though we encourage right behaviors in ourselves and society. Laws are provided to enforce right behaviors and punish crime. And though punishment follows lawlessness, misdeeds may not be corrected fully.

Upon what can we rely as a rock solid foundation, because what matters to you and me, matters most first of all?

This is where authentic faith comes alive, proven and active.

Faith Matters

Those readers who know me, and perhaps you are one, realize that I have purposefully chosen to align with Jesus Christ and His teachings.

History proves His existence and an empty grave proves His power. I have visited the empty tomb many times, and I can testify that indeed there is no body there!

I choose to believe because of the witnesses of those who have studied and gone before, including many who have set out to disprove the facts in scripture, and particularly the resurrection, and come away as believers. Please see the recommended reading portion of this book where some of these resources for study are listed, out of millions from which to choose.

I do not, nor will I ever "know it all." That fact, however, is not a reason to disbelieve or discredit what I have not actually witnessed or experienced. It is not my intention to deny or discredit anyone's faith or experience. Faith is personal and it is cherished. It is acted upon when proven authentic and true.

Herein rests the Breakthrough so many desire. Maybe you are one. It's a worthy goal to seek more knowledge and seek God in the process, studying and drawing your conclusions.

Glen Aubrey

Truth, real truth, welcomes investigation. It never shrinks from those who wish to discover.

So carry on. Be encouraged. Learn much. May your faith grow and may your faith in God grow as well because faith matters.

> Truth, real truth, welcomes investigation. It never shrinks from those who wish to discover.

Chapter 2
The Desire for a Breakthrough

How much do you desire a Breakthrough? It pays to know the answer to this question, and know why you answer it in the way you do.

You are asked to define a Breakthrough for you. It is necessary to see where and how you fit as an individual in your relationships with others, at home, at work, in all your networks.

In the **Leadership Trilogy for Business Core Team Development**, structures called Core Teams are defined and explored. The Leadership Trilogy consists of three books (see **Products and Services** and this website **www.CreativeTeamPublishing.com**):

1. *Leadership Is ... How to Build Your Legacy*
2. *Industrial Strength Solutions ... Build Successful Work Teams!*
3. *Core Teams Work ... Their Principles and Practices*

In brief, the Core Team is a work structure uniquely defined by the people who make up the team, who agree on shared values and strive to live by them, unreservedly. You are invited to review the term, 'Core Team' as an acronym in this table below:

The Core Team: A Functioning Workable Solution (Table) *Industrial Strength Solutions:*

C: Consistency

O: Obedience to Shared Values

R: Right Relationships

E: Example

T: Trust

E: Essentials of Composite Nature

A: Accountability

M: Method

© 2012 and 2019 by Glen Aubrey. All Rights Reserved.

Faith Matters

The Core Team helps anyone define what they truly desire and the reasons they desire it, both as an individual and as part of the team.

Additionally, you are asked to personally consider four life-changing questions.

The **Four Questions** from *Leadership Is…* are uniquely tied to **Values, Vision, Mission, and Message,** from the same book. These are primary considerations for any individual or team, leader or follower.

Here are **Values, Vision, Mission, and Message,** defined:

1. *Values* constitute the core principles upon which agreement exists between leader and follower and are made up of intangibles that never change.

2. *Vision* describes an overall purpose, the reasons why actions are considered, and the hopes for what the future can be in goal accomplishment. Through vision, cause and motive give meaning to activity.

3. *Mission* is made up of the tasks to complete, the methods used to achieve their goals, the evaluations that show success or failure, and the tangible rewards to be received when the mission is accomplished.

4. *Message* represents life-lessons learned through the fulfillment of the mission that impact people with truth. Message is the acquired knowledge that is applied with wisdom.

And here are **The Four Questions:**

1. **Who are you at your core?**
   *This is a question of **values**.* This question seeks to know the heart-core of the individual, what makes them tick, what are their principled, unchangeable, bedrock beliefs upon which their entire world-view and actions are based. These values will likely include, but not be limited to, intangibles of integrity, trust, commitment, faithfulness, respect, cooperation, and love.

2. **What are you called to accomplish?**
   *This is a question of **vision**.* Vision gives purpose. Where this question is answered with a list of tangibles, a person is veering off course. Accomplishments are heart-related when they seek to build up other people and accomplish goals through investment. Vision is best described in intangibles. When someone answering refers to benefits seen in values as opposed to benefits seen in valuables, the question and answer are hitting home.

3. **What do you want?**

    *This is a question of **mission**.* Mission is composed of actions to fulfill a goal. Accomplishment is seen in the effects, both materially and within a frame of mind. What anyone who desires personal growth wants should be in direct correlation to their answers to the first two questions. Mission will include hard work and the satisfaction coming from completing a job well. Happiness should be evidenced in tangible rewards—the products of achievement—along with intangible inner repose—an assurance of attainment, a healthy sense of pride in the fulfillment of purpose.

4. **Whom will you impact?**

    *This is a question of **message**.* Lessons learned are worth little until they become operative in real life. People long for and appreciate authenticity when actions verify words. People who are impacted for good because of a follower's or leader's life model can find themselves in a state of receptivity for learning what, how, and why something or someone worked. Principled truth that invades and transforms life makes people take notice, and for those who desire more than mediocrity, it creates hunger for more of whatever "that" is and wherever "it" came from. Message is seen through measures and methods. Message is enfolded into desires, decisions, and deeds. The life-lessons learned and taught to those who observe and want to receive them, become the message.

Use Values, Vision, Mission, and Message, and their related Four Questions as standards of measurement if you agree. Use them as tools of self-discovery and improvement.

*****

Life-change for growth often rests on what you want and why you want it. Further, what you want is shaped by your beliefs and practices. If you are part of a Core Team, that association carries responsibilities in your actions because they impact others on the team. If you are not part of a team, you still need to determine where you fit because of desire and belief, because you affect others, regardless.

Your beliefs and practices give birth to additional actions driven by motives you deem worthy as you weigh options and opportunities. Put another way, motives birth methods and methods produce consequences.

> Life-change for growth often rests on what you want and why you want it.

I used to tell my children as they were growing up, "Make good choices and good things happen; make bad choices and bad things happen."

Faith Matters

We know it may not be all that simple, but the central truth remains: choices count.

> Motives birth methods and methods produce consequences.

Several years ago a highly successful businessman reached out to me because he determined that I would benefit from his counsel, business acumen, experience, and friendship. He was right, and I was hungry for what he knew about business and wise marketplace choices. I valued his camaraderie, too.

He was generous with his time and often contributed his money, too; and he highly admired and valued my creative writing and music expertise.

As we grew to know each other better, I offered to donate performances of music to him because he valued this music so much. And enjoy it he did! He visited recording sessions and it became a real personal delight to perform and record music in his presence and share music with him he could not purchase because this was a gift.

We were enjoying beverages at one point and he casually but intentionally mentioned, "I'm rich," He was. What he wanted, as shown by actions and words, was "more." He simply could not refuse the next big business deal to make additional money, and it was usually in large amounts.

So while he was generous, and I was grateful and tried to reciprocate, he was also a product of his own greed. That is not criticizing; it was just a fact. He was proud of his achievements in the corporate world and in real estate. Should his motive for desiring more be unearthed, it could truthfully be said that he greatly valued financial and business successes almost to a fault.

When he died suddenly, all of his accumulated assets were no longer his to enjoy. Such is the state for everyone at death. There comes an end to acquisition. What is left must be distributed.

That true story revealed one man's true desires, motives, and results. Our desires, motives, and results are revealed in our life's stories, too.

> Our desires, motives, and results are revealed in our life's stories.

So back to the question: what do you want? In the context of The Four Questions, this is question number three, following two which deal with the intangible of who persons believe themselves to be, and the tangible of what they believe they may be called to accomplish.

Question number four asks who will be impacted by the person's answers to the first three questions. The point is this: personhood, calling, and desires shall not be hidden; rather, they will be shared if a person is to "be the servant" of all, as Jesus taught.

Mark 9:35 (NIV):

Sitting down, Jesus called the Twelve and said, "Anyone who wants to be first must be the very last, and the servant of all."

> Greatness is evidenced in service, not because of rank or success, but because of a sincere desire to obey and become a resource to others who have need.

True desires are seen in how one who has acquired much uses what he or she has amassed to help and assist others. "To whom much is given, much will be required." That phrase is recorded in **Luke 12:48b (NIV)** and this scripture shows us a piece of God's economy:

"From everyone who has been given much, much will be demanded; and from the one who has been entrusted with much, much more will be asked."

The verse speaks of willing obedience to higher authority, a recognition of moral values, and an honest desire to give from a heart submissive to God's commands, learning how best to use what is given to help others.

The verse refers to far more than financial wealth; it refers to how one who has been blessed becomes the giver of blessings to others, especially if the receiver doesn't even know the giver.

> True desires are seen in how one who has acquired much uses what he or she has amassed to help and assist others.

I've been on both sides, as receiver and giver. And it is more blessed to give than receive. From the testimony of the Apostle Paul, quoted in **Acts 20:35 (NIV)**:

> "In everything I did, I showed you that by this kind of hard work we must help the weak, remembering the words the Lord Jesus himself said: 'It is more blessed to give than to receive.'"

It is good to desire more for the right reasons; it is even better to give as much as possible. You likely have heard this: "Make all you can. Save all you can. Give away all you can." Doesn't it all rest on motive? In other words, why you want what you want is important because of what you intend to do with all you acquire.

So how is this related to authentic faith? The Breakthrough of authentic faith and the realization that faith matters take the idea of acquisition and motive to a whole new level. Acquisition accompanied by unhealthy pride in achievement can distort faith. This condition supposedly teaches that faith may not be needed in some endeavors at all, and that self-sufficiency can take charge, resulting in arrogance.

> Why you want what you want is important because of what you intend to do with all you acquire.

Knowing and accepting you are not ultimately in charge, that you desire to be a giver at heart, may open up vast opportunities to you if you are blessed with resources. Let your desire be to know how to willingly and gratefully share what you possess, and be generous.

It's a way of living and it doesn't always mean smooth sailing, free of life's storms. The reality is this: bad times can come to good and generous people … we know this, and may have experienced rough seas, or may be acquainted with people who have gone through, or are going through, difficult circumstances or events. This causes us to ask, "What are our reactions to difficulty?"

One of our Creative Team Publishing authors is Robert F. Dees, Major General, U.S. Army, Retired. His message is one of resilience in a relationship with Jesus Christ.

~ (See Robert F. Dees' books at **https://resiliencegodstyle.com**)

Resilience in tough times is possible when one's faith is anchored firmly on a rock of truth, where reliance upon God is central no matter what the conditions are.

We push forward and rise above difficulty through reliance upon God, faith in His provision, often requiring hard work for a higher cause. Determination is not optional when one knows that what is desired is birthed on a solid belief, proven and therefore unshakeable, no matter what.

> Resilience in tough times is possible when one's faith is anchored firmly on a rock of truth, where reliance upon God is central no matter what the conditions are.

What are your reasons for desiring a Breakthrough? What does it look like to you?

I am convinced that our God-authored Breakthroughs are directly tied to authentic faith, and that this alliance includes our willful obedience and submission to God, often including hard work, full submission to His will, and desiring Him be "in charge" and the source of all we want and need.

Faith Matters

How can we receive and dwell in more authentic faith, appropriately positioned as a follower of Christ? Certainly the answer includes: by listening to God's message of truth, and willfully following and obeying God's revealed will, seeking Him more.

Romans 10:17 (NIV):

Consequently, faith comes from hearing the message, and the message is heard through the word about Christ.

Faith is active when we choose to activate it. It is prayer in action when we trust in God's provision.

It is our lifestyle when we choose to make it so. It is evidenced in our words, deeds, motives, and methods.

Our place may not be to understand fully, but to follow wholeheartedly because we know we are anchored to Christ without reservation.

Chapter 3
Authentic Faith in Action

Many are the activities and events I do not control. Some I don't desire to control! Our task is not to enumerate and dwell on those; rather, to see what I do control and how I accept my responsibilities, again seeking to follow God's desires relating to the items that have been placed in my charge.

In a quest for significance and success, a gentleman I'd known for a long period, rose to a position of top leadership, power, and influence in a well-respected organization which employed and impacted many. He also served on the board of a non-profit, charitable organization whose primary task was to help other charities chart improvements in staff relations, team building, and organizational outcomes.

From outside observance, this alignment of person, charity, and responsibility seemed nearly picture perfect. All the trappings of balancing success were there.

As years went by, a deeper and flawed character was observed by people close to him. It was disturbing.

It was seen in his personal communications or the lack of them, overt desires to achieve and acquire loftier positions, many of which alienated friends, even family. These new conditions didn't correspond with this gentleman's generous contributions.

These inconsistencies became increasingly frequent in character and activity, and doors of communication appeared to shut or become difficult to open. Still maintaining a friendship at least in passing, the depths of relationships others had enjoyed with him dissolved for many. I was one of them.

These relationship departures were hard to explain, and some never could be. They did not abate; rather, increased as additional years went by.

People choose to alter behaviors and opinions over time, of course, due to many factors, some of which are in their control, and others which are not. Altered behaviors are what demonstrate sincerity of internal change. People who are manifesting increasing responsibility for their own actions, including speech, are those others can see are undergoing consistent, maturing character growth.

In this case, instead, people who thought they knew the individual were frustrated by his presentation of two versions of himself. Which was the real one?

Faith Matters

Authentic faith is demonstrated in authentic faithfulness regardless of circumstances including what may come across as expedient or necessary at any given time. Alterations of character should not become examples of repositioning, or take the place of friendships grounded in faith, hope, and love.

> Authentic faith is demonstrated in authentic faithfulness regardless of circumstances including what may come across as expedient or necessary at any given time.

In contrast, another friend over even more years never altered his character. This kind of consistency built more depth in our relationship and a "You can be counted on" kind of mutual friendship. No matter what occurred, the friendship was present and active, and it still is even to this day.

Not nearly as much power and position in his life and life's work, but reliability in long-lasting depths of friendship were the hallmarks of a long standing relationship. Which would you prefer if not earnestly desire?

> Alterations of character should not become examples of repositioning, or take the place of friendships grounded in faith, hope, and love.

A personal choice of responsibility should remain constant and faithful through all of life's courses. Is it possible to achieve? I believe the answer is a resounding "Yes." This is not something accomplished through sheer willpower alone; though determination is needed. It is achieved through humbly choosing to follow God's consistent patterns of how He treats those who follow Him, and endeavoring to model what He demonstrates.

Perfection in everything probably is not an achievable goal even though Jesus, Himself, delivered an injunction to "be perfect." The context of His comments is showing love with limits or restrictions. Perhaps real and achievable perfection includes removing those restrictions, a willful action as an exercise of authentic faith.

Matthew 5:46-48 (NIV), quoting Jesus:

> [46] "If you love those who love you, what reward will you get? Are not even the tax collectors doing that? [47] And if you greet only your own people, what are you doing more than others? Do not even pagans do that? [48] Be perfect, therefore, as your heavenly Father is perfect."

This teaching has to do with heart *and* hands, thoughts and intentions as well as activity. Apart from His presence in us and our willful obedience to His ways and commands, we cannot even begin to follow as we should. Heart and hands have to link because we choose to join them.

Now I am not setting myself up as one who has achieved authentic faith consistently or even partially. Is that ever true! I've made many errors, and have desired to sincerely apologize for my mistakes.

Authentic faith is most readily seen in both desire and deeds. Confession plays a role, too. Where faults and mistakes occur, and they will, we are enjoined to admit and own them, and make them right.

From **James 5:16 (KJV)**

[16] Confess your faults one to another, and pray one for another, that ye may be healed. The effectual fervent prayer of a righteous man availeth much.

> Authentic faith is most readily seen in both desire and deeds. Confession plays a role, too.

Confession includes healing and a restoration of relationships as well as forgiveness for negative deeds and their side effects. Confession also comes with prayer for each other expressed from those who are in right standing with God (righteous). In fact, these elements are inseparable.

My actions are born of my character. Yours are, too. While we may not achieve ultimate perfection we *can* choose right direction. If intents and motives are just, our actions will be affected and our worlds will see.

Examples:

1. If you make a promise, keep your promise.
2. Tell the truth.
3. Show kindness.
4. Exercise humility.
5. Be one on whom others can count.
6. Fulfill duties to which you commit in ways that exceed expectations.
7. Do this because you want to, not because you have to.

When errors occur, embrace the opportunity to humble yourself, own your part, and make right what you did that was deemed or proven wrong.

> Faithfulness means consistency of character without compromise, positive attitudes, and words proven by deeds.

Daily, in virtually all we do, we are presented with opportunities and options of making these good choices.

Chapter 4
Undeniable Facts

I have come to realize some undeniable facts. I am still venturing down the path of coming to grips with conditions of my existence, good and bad, those that are present and prevalent whether or not I will them to be. While not "in charge" of most, I am completely responsible for my reactions to events that occur. Part of exercising authentic faith is acting responsibly in these circumstances.

The undeniable facts are these: you own responsibility for your reactions just like I do for mine. Far from concluding imposed negatives, conditions good and bad represent golden opportunities to let the light of Christ and His love shine through, regardless.

Certainly this truth involves observance, acceptance of His will, submission often, and may include strong desires to help create solid improvements if and when possible. You know the phrase, "It is what it is." I don't use the offensive language of the *Urban Dictionary* in translating or employing this phrase, and I am definitely not always resigned to the inevitability of negative circumstances, that just because something is wrong, it has to remain so.

I believe that undeniable facts can include strong desires and activity on my part to correct errant behaviors and promote positive results. Where positive change is desired, commensurate actions can follow, and responsibilities often increase.

> The undeniable facts are these: you own responsibility for your reactions just like I do for mine.

I am quite aware I cannot alter everything, but I can contribute to changes over which I do have influence and possibly control. The question that arises is, "How much effort do I choose to exert, to create positive improvements in conditions and behaviors, including mine, and am I willing to expend the sufficient effort which often includes sacrifice in the endeavor?"

I am fully aware that just because I *want* improvements and choose to work hard to achieve them, I am not promised guarantees of success in implementation and results. I am also aware that other people involved may not share my commitment levels to initiation and follow-through in quests to achieve desired results, and that if I choose to work with others, I often will need to lead or influence them as well as try to inspire them. I also must choose to willingly value them more than just their function or what they can do for me and my desires.

Faith Matters

It's also an undeniable fact that people are more important than what they do. I have believed and taught this truth for almost all of my adult life. Put another way, relationships come before and give birth to function.

> Relationships come before and give birth to function.

I define a "relationship" as the choice I make about other people's success, changing my behavior to help them win. Function consists of the actions I choose to validate my desires to build strong relationships.

> It's also an undeniable fact that people are more important than what they do.

I've encountered leaders who say to me, "What you are advocating is not real life." In one instance I replied to an employer, "It may not be real life *yet*, but it is real direction."

Let me tell you this true story. Conflict was occurring fairly often in the organization because the leader did not value the people who worked in his company any more than what they were able to provide as their function. His attitude was that people were of no more worth than what they could do.

I completely disagreed, and expressed this view to him, with respect for him and his position; but we never agreed.

It didn't surprise me much at all when he left the organization a few months after I had departed, that relational vacuums were prevalent and that positive and enduring team function born of, and borne on, selfless giving and strong relationships was not present.

Conversations with him had been guarded at best and unpleasant at worst. There were many. This state of affairs reminded me of another undeniable fact: you cannot alter other people's beliefs and behaviors. Unless they are open to hearing and responding to views that may differ from their own, it's fruitless effort.

Also, it became undeniably clear that it may be completely fruitless to try and continue working with those who practice sheer and unbending recalcitrance to the people-are-more-important-than-function principle and practices, whether leaders or followers. Sometimes, if after repeated tries it is simply not working, it may be simply best to depart in peace. I did.

> You cannot alter other people's beliefs and behaviors.
> Unless they become open to hearing and responding to
> views that may differ from their own,
> it's fruitless effort.

But *if* there are those with whom working together is possible in and through building strong relationships and personal values-driven behaviors, I may want to request their help in achieving worthwhile endeavors, to help correct wrongs and promote positive results.

One more undeniable fact: if the cause is worth it, and you and I sincerely believe in its value, then we have the option and possibly an obligation to choose to give it our all, regardless of the impediments or struggles we may encounter.

This is a gentle combination of willpower and submissive willingness that helps a worthwhile cause become reality. Belief, commensurate bold action, genuine care, and sensitivity are required.

> There is a gentle combination of willpower and submissive willingness that helps any worthwhile cause become reality. Belief, commensurate bold action, genuine care, and sensitivity are required.

These are undeniable facts.

Jesus instituted this model of behavior. He ministered to people because He loved them, regardless of their function or misdeeds.

Glen Aubrey

We can't earn His grace and love: they are gifts. Even when we were unworthy, Christ died for us. His love for us meant His willing sacrifice for us.

His desire for relationship with us birthed His function toward us. When we desire to follow Him, we choose this model of living to emulate, and we do this by willfully submitting to Him and His ways, serving others.

The song, **His Love for Us** expresses God's love given to us. I composed the music and lyrics in the 70s, and Paul Mickelson beautifully arranged the song for choir. It was published by Lillenas Publishing Company in November, 1977 as part of their Evangel Choir series. It was reassigned to me in April, 1984.

His Love for Us

© 1977 Lillenas Publishing Company. Reassigned to Glen Aubrey, 1984.
© 2019 Glen Aubrey. All Rights Reserved.

Have you ever wondered why Jesus came to die?
Have you ever wondered why there's an empty tomb?
Could it be that we were worthy of all of this?
No, it was all because God loved us.

His love for us sent Jesus to the cross;
His love for us raised Him from the grave.
No greater love will we ever know;
This love has pow'r to save.

Faith Matters

It reaches to the base of human need:
That from all sin and death we must be freed!
The cross and empty tomb of Jesus
Proclaim that love will free us!

God's love does free us and allows us to experience His Breakthrough when we, by faith, accept His provision in Christ, given through God's grace.
There is no other way to experience a true Breakthrough.

Chapter 5
As an Example

The question never is *if* we show an example. The question always is, "What kind?" Our lives are examples of what we believe and value. We need to inquire of ourselves often, as a part of honest self-assessment, "What does the example I show demonstrate?"

This 'example' truth was incorporated into our corporate and government Creative Team Resources Group (CTRG) training and consultation (www.ctrg.com). The 'E' in Core of Core Team addressed it. (See page 56 of this book.)

Sometimes the most profound truths I desire to express are best articulated through my music. This has been a preference and pattern for years, since high school and even earlier.

The year was 1973, and I wrote **As an Example**. The song is a prayer really, and for a young college student, it came from my heart and soul, a part of my personal faith journey. The song was utilized in churches and by small music groups. I share the music and lyrics with you.

As an Example

Music Transcription: Harvey Tellinghuisen.
© 2019 Glen Aubrey. All Rights Reserved.

Faith Matters

Glen Aubrey

As an Example

Words and music © 1973 Glen Aubrey. All Rights Reserved.

Help me to live the kind of life
That is pleasing, Lord, in Your sight.
Out of gratitude for all You have done,
Help me live the life You've given
In the footsteps of Your Son.

As an example to my brother,
Help me live in Your Spirit,
Empowered each day.

As an example to my neighbor,
Help me live so that he
Will see Your pow'r in me,
And want to find out
Just what it's all about.

Help me, O Lord, in life to share
Your unfailing love ev'rywhere.
Out of gratitude for all You have done,
Help me live a life that's holy
In the footsteps of Your Son.

As an Example to my brother,
Help me serve in Your Spirit,
Empowered each day.
As an Example to my neighbor,

Faith Matters

> Help me live so that he
> Will see Your love in me,
> And want to find out
> Just what it's all about.

The lyrics contain these truths:

1. We *want* to live our lives in submission to God because *this is pleasing to Him*.
2. We endeavor to live for God because *we are grateful* for all He has done and is doing.
3. We *actively request His help* in all we do, in full submission to Him.
4. This is about *following Jesus without any reservations*.
5. It's possible to live for God, giving Him complete control, *when we strive to live according to His Spirit working in us*.
6. This is *the example we want to show our worlds*.
7. *We desire to showcase God's power at work in us*.
8. This is *obedience to God in real life*.
9. When people see God's power genuinely active in our lives, they will yearn to *find out what it's all about*.
10. The *unfailing Love of God* is the most gracious gift we can share, because God demonstrated His love to us in Christ. Again, it is His gift of grace, which we receive by faith, even though unmerited.
11. We *share the love* He has given us.

12. *Holiness*, defined as being set apart for good works in service, *is possible* when we yield to God completely, following the example of Christ.
13. Often we become *God's vessels of change* as we seek to be an example, empowered by His Holy Spirit.
14. We want to live so that those around us will see *authentic faith in action* and want to discover more.

When I examine my levels of faith, I am reminded that it's fruitless to offer God excuses if I try to go it alone. He knows my occasional tendencies to retake control, even when I know deep down that relinquishing my personal clutch and opening my hands and heart to allow Him to lead, are the right things to do.

No struggle; rather, willing submission. The two cannot coexist simultaneously. This journey is one He authors, not me. I need to remember that.

The next chapter may help to define and demonstrate authentic faith more.

Chapter 6
The Practice of Faith

Authentic faith is simple to relate: it is willfully putting God in control. I believe actually doing this can become complicated if not quite difficult when our desires do not align with His and we insist on doing it our way instead of obeying.

Sometimes we put barriers in the way of understanding and accomplishing letting go, and it is we who must remove the inhibitors if we choose to do so. God rarely removes the barriers miraculously that we need to act on ourselves.

Here are seven steps for us to consider:

1. First, *read and study* scriptures on authentic faith. Refer to them often. Memorize them. Write them down. Some are listed here on the next few pages.
2. Pray and ask God to *open your eyes of understanding*.
3. In prayer, earnestly tell God you *want* Him to lead you, and be *open* to His truth, revealed both in scripture and in council from godly people in your life who showcase an evidence of faith.
4. *Accept* what scripture says without reservation.

5. Write down the areas you control and talk to God about each, *offering each to Him,* and ask Him to take charge. By "take charge" I don't mean an abdication of responsibility: I'm referring to willfully letting God lead. Then *choose to follow,* understanding that following may and likely will mean willfully assuming responsibilities He has for us.
6. *Align your life with His example* and *change your behavior.*
7. *Thank Him* for leading you as you grow in authentic faith.

Here's a scripture for your reference and use. This one would be good to memorize. **Hebrews 11:6 (NIV)**:

> And without faith it is impossible to please God, because anyone who comes to him must believe that he exists and that he rewards those who earnestly seek him.

The sequence is important. Authentic faith begins with belief in God's existence and that He has the desire and power to reward those who earnestly seek Him. Without this kind of faith it is impossible to please God. It's a question of pure alignment, no distractions.

The role of faith is crucial, too. Authentic faith is evidenced in actions and behaviors, not just merely talking about God and belief.

James 2:26 (NIV) is succinct:

> As the body without the spirit is dead, so faith without deeds is dead.

If action doesn't follow a declaration of belief, the Bible indicates that faith has died. Here is **James 2:17 (KJV)**:

> Even so faith, if it hath not works, is dead, being alone.

This is real isolation, separate existence, sheer aloneness. Faith and deeds must be connected if one is to support the other and if either is genuine. They do not exist independently.

James 2:17 (NIV):

> In the same way, faith by itself, if it is not accompanied by action, is dead.

The practice of authentic faith, because faith matters, is seen in altered behaviors in alignment with God's will and His plans. No meaningless talk here; rather, observable action.

A Christ follower's beliefs, whether verbalized or not, are seen in a Christ follower's actions. No exceptions, no excuses.

> Faith and deeds must be connected if one is to support the other and if either is genuine.
> They do not exist independently.

There appears to be no "wiggle room" that allows faith and deeds to not match. The Bible appears to very clear on that.

> A Christ follower's beliefs whether verbalized or not, are seen in a Christ follower's actions.
> No exceptions, no excuses.

I recommend a Bible study program that an interested person should access: https://www.biblegateway.com. Type 'faith' in the search box and discover 458 related Bible verses beginning in Genesis and ending in Revelation. Note that 'faith' and 'faithfulness' are intertwined in many. On top of this, discover 98 references in the Topical Index.

These many references reaffirm the importance of what we are calling authentic faith and the faithful action that must accompany it.

Talk about inspiring; you are invited to review **Hebrews Chapter 11 (NIV)**, often called the "Faith Chapter" or "Faith in Action."

These many references reaffirm the importance of what we are calling authentic faith and the faithful action that must accompany it.

Below is the writer's list of **"The Heroes of Faith"** from **Chapter 11**.

> These many references reaffirm the importance of what we are calling authentic faith and the faithful action that must accompany it.

Bible students will instantly recognize these names and associated stories. Talk about evidence:

"Abel, Enoch, Noah, Sarah..."

Note **verse 13:**

"All these people were still living by faith when they died. They did not receive the things promised; they only saw them and welcomed them from a distance, admitting that they were foreigners and strangers on earth."

The list continues:

"Abraham, Isaac, Jacob and Esau in regard to their future; Joseph, Moses' parents, Moses," and this amazing demonstration:

[30] "By faith the walls of Jericho fell, after the army had marched around them for seven days. [31] By faith the prostitute Rahab, because she welcomed the spies, was not killed with those who were disobedient."

In summary:

[32] "And what more shall I say? I do not have time to tell about Gideon, Barak, Samson and Jephthah, about David and Samuel and the prophets, [33] who through faith conquered kingdoms, administered justice, and gained what was promised."

Note **verse 39** (<u>underlining and italic emphasis by author</u>):

[39] "These were all <u>commended</u> for their faith, yet none of them received what had been promised, [40] since God had planned something better <u>for us</u> so that <u>only *together with us*</u> would they be made <u>perfect</u>."

Faith Matters

Bottom line: All of us are *united* in authentic faith with those who have gone before who exercised that faith. <u>God commends them and us</u>.

All are proofs that authentic faith works, and is seen in the faithfulness of those who believe, both historically and currently.

Faith is *the* common characteristic that binds generations in belief and practice, *not* necessarily a fulfillment for those who exercise authentic faith while living.

We who live in post-New Testament times can clearly see where fulfillment occurred from stories of the patriarchs' beliefs and practices. We are charged to exercise the same kind of authentic faith whether or not we see fulfillment in our lifetimes.

> We are charged to exercise ... authentic faith whether or not we see fulfillment in our lifetimes.

We see authentic faith at work in the lives of people who are fully submitted to God, His promises, and purposes. <u>That *is* the Breakthrough</u>!

Authentic faith is evidenced in principle and practice. We can share in this faith if we so choose.

> We see authentic faith at work in the lives of people who are fully submitted to God, His promises, and purposes.
> <u>That *is* the Breakthrough</u>!
> Authentic faith is evidenced in principle and practice.
> We can share in this faith if we so choose.

Authentic Faith Touches Other People in Need through Us

Not too long ago I listened to, and thoroughly enjoyed a presentation at my church. The topic was the story of the Good Samaritan, a story which is known by many. It is recorded in **Luke 10:25-37**.

The presenter helped his listeners identify who our "neighbors" really are. Often they may be individuals others may simply ignore or "pass by" in times of trial or trouble.

In scripture, Jesus' telling of this story, or parable clearly indicated that for us to be willing to follow His example and give unreservedly, we should not just pass by when we see obvious need; rather, we must go beyond what may or may not be expected to assist someone else, whether or not the person in need is "likeable" and "acceptable" to us.

Our obedience to meeting needs beyond our own becomes a true testimony of God's faithfulness and the compassion of Jesus exercised *through us*. Christ healed wounds across the spectrum of need; we should be willing to do this, too. It's another example of faith and deeds cooperating together.

This truth causes us to ask, "Who needs my touch today? If I am an example for Him as a Christ-follower, what are my responsibilities to reach out and help other people in times of need?"

I must recognize that doing so may "cost" me something, and it very likely will. Is that a cost I am willing to embrace?

Helping others in times of trial or test are actions where the Word of Christ dwelling in me becomes flesh in my activities.

How committed am I to say, "I see the needs. Send me to meet them."

God works through us when we are willing to be used of Him to touch others as another example of connecting faith and deeds.

Chapter 7
Some Things Matter, Some Things Don't

Digital technology is a tool. How it's used and for what motives can make all the difference.

Spend any time in front of your computer or using your smart phone, and you may be bombarded with ads uniquely placed and specifically designed for your profile, based on personal buying preferences and actual purchases.

Truthfully, these ads can help us make good choices. They can also become annoying distractions for those who may not want their favorite program or sports event to be interrupted for even a minute in an effort to sell them something.

Technology is welcomed when used appropriately. One example: the digital age has opened brand new doors to gathering information from across the world about how God is moving and changing lives. This is welcome news!

We are no longer blocked from access to unlimited information if we are "connected." How we utilize the information available to us, and what information we seek, are choices we make.

Truth matters. Faith matters. It's all about **Faith Matters** and God's unshakeable provision for us if we trust Him willfully. When one walks according to His design, the desire is to use rightly the tools before us, including those of the digital age in which we all now live.

What garners your attention within the vast digital opportunities for communication, gaming, and gathering information?

One of my family members recently observed that in today's digital worlds, very little personal information remains permanently inaccessible from view or unable to be viewed by someone. Rarely can anyone dwell in protected isolation if "connected."

Think about financial transactions, bank records, credit and debit card numbers, social security details, medical records, and virtually all correspondence. On one side, everything digital can be hacked, or so it seems. We hear about cyber criminals on the news weekly, even daily, penetrating virtually everything including energy grids, banking institutions, government records, food supply, and water.

Faith Matters

What happened to assured protection of privacy? It is not nearly as possible as it once was, or privacy is at least difficult to set up and maintain.

Laws are continuously upgraded, but people's characters are forever governed by choices and why the choices are made. Some people choose to violate others. Unfortunately, fraud and stealing are rampant. Others make good and godly choices following God's designs.

Breaches require fixing, of course. Fixing can consume valuable time, cause frustrating inconveniences, and worse. Security firms make huge money selling software and subscriptions to protect your information. In the United States, countless laws are in place and new ones emerge regularly to enshrine freedoms of speech and press, and protect the private information of citizens. Yet violations of "personal space" occur almost unabated. When criminals are caught, more come around. The trend never ceases.

Do you wonder *why* misuses of digital technology and violations of laws appear to be growing? There may be a simple answer: one friend expressed that nothing really is new and the numbers of violations of law may not actually be growing at all. We simply have the ability to become aware of them more readily.

Personal activities and those of others simply could not be found as easily as discovery makes possible in the digital age. Years ago access to information on criminal activity, or any activity for that matter, was not as readily viewable. She may have a point.

Blessings and harm grow together with ever more rapid paces given the speed and easy access of digital information. This truth is demonstrated once again: what we do with any technology is our responsibility.

Laws are designed to protect persons from anyone who would steal what is not rightly theirs. But as in every age, "thieves break through and steal."

The Bible offers assurances to one who trusts God and lives in authentic faith. Jesus addressed the issue of where we store what is valuable to us.

See **Matthew 6: 19, 20 (NIV)**:

"[19] Do not store up for yourselves treasures on earth, where moths and vermin destroy, and where thieves break in and steal. [20] But store up for yourselves treasures in heaven, where moths and vermin do not destroy, and where thieves do not break in and steal."

God's economy includes recognition of our personal worth across the spectrum. His records for you and me are eternal. They cannot be touched by those who would steal or try to misuse information. That is why it is wise to store up treasures in heaven. It was true when Jesus said it, and it's true today.

By faith we accept this truth and express confidence in God. While it likely is wise and advisable for us to change online passwords on a regular basis, God's recognition of us and our faith is vital, secure, and more valuable than any of man's devices. No "passwords" are required to live in God's protection except His grace and our acceptance of His provision.

It's true that some things matter and some things don't. Whom do you trust? In terms of what really lasts, where is your primary focus?

Living in fear of people who may try to steal what is ours, is one option and not a very good one in my view. Another option is to be mindful and try to protect yourself, those you love, and others entrusted to your care, but realize that even our best efforts can fail.

Storing up treasures in heaven requires right and lawful activities on earth with godly and unselfish intent. Authentic faith confirms that God has our best interests at heart. He will protect what really matters, and authentic faith matters, matter!

Human laws and efforts can and should be engaged to counteract criminals and protect the innocent. But when it comes to real security and wellbeing with guarantees for the future, no one is more trustworthy than God.

Believe this and trust God completely, and your soul will be comforted no matter what happens on earth.

Of course, we realize that not everyone shares the dedication to treasuring individual values and valuables. Insecure and selfish individuals may go to great lengths to violate a friend, coworker, acquaintance, or neighbor in an effort of selfish gain, no matter who they hurt. That truth has been present since Adam and Eve, Cain and Abel. Remember: their story is where we first learn of one being murdered because of jealousy and greed. Evil is real, and God is real.

> Authentic faith confirms that God has our best interests at heart. He will protect what really matters, and authentic faith matters, matter!

What matters most is what and whom we hold dear and close. Many would say family and friends are treasures to be held close, and certainly truth resides in that answer. Followers of Christ hold authentic faith in God and His provision very close in all of life's dealings. He honors investments in His name and in support of His cause.

Faith Matters

No one can violate or steal eternal values-driven behaviors and the results. God's provision is secure. We can rest in that truth.

Where you and I place our trust is important. It would take two hands at least, to count the number of bank failures in Southern California during the last twenty years. The best news is this: God never fails.

You and I can trust Him. He is never short changed, robbed, nor is He the victim of crime. He never comes up short. Plus, He never violates His perfect will.

When Jesus died and rose from the grave, eternal life was guaranteed for those who accept his gift of grace through faith. The promises of God's faithfulness have always been fulfilled and always will be. The future is certain for those who trust in Him and obey His commands.

> What really counts and matters most is what and whom we hold dear and close.

Yes, we should be mindful of the present, realizing that both good and evil exist, but we should continually trust God for the things that really matter, like Faith, Hope, and Love.

A verse many know is **John 3:16 (KJV)**:

For God so loved the world, that he gave his only begotten Son, that whosoever believeth in him should not perish, but have everlasting life.

The promise of life comes with God's personal guarantee. That promise cost Him his Son who died for us and rose again. No one can violate or steal authentic faith in Christ's provision.

Are you persuaded to place your highest trust in God's care and provision? The writer of Romans was.

Romans 8:38, 39 (KJV):

[38] For I am persuaded, that neither death, nor life, nor angels, nor principalities, nor powers, nor things present, nor things to come, [39] Nor height, nor depth, nor any other creature, shall be able to separate us from the love of God, which is in Christ Jesus our Lord.

As was stated at the beginning of this chapter, truth matters. Faith matters. It's all about **Faith Matters** and God's unshakeable provision for us if we believe and desire to live for Him. He helps us focus on eternal values and what's really important, and helps us live according to His plans and His will when we seek Him.

Chapter 8
Break Through!

Think about the future. Even when we plan carefully and methodically, what has not been *actually experienced yet* represents vast unknowns. We find it difficult to accept what we have not already walked through, such as circumstances and events still to come, great or small. Anticipation of what may occur can be accompanied by negatives like doubt, fear, anxiety, and just plain old worry.

On a brighter side, our futures can also be opportunities to experience hope and confident assurance when authentic faith in God is present and exercised willfully, without reservation.

We read that God is love. Love is His character and method of operation. Therefore, we need to accept through faith that God loves us, and that He is fully in control.

Because He loves, we trust, not trying to run our lives in spite of what His will is. His love and our trust, or faith and confidence in Him, go hand in hand.

See **1 John 4:8 (NIV):**

"Whoever does not love does not know God, because God is love."

> Because He loves, we trust, not trying to run our lives in spite of what His will is. His love and our trust, or faith and confidence in Him, go hand in hand.

Love is God's core trait. We're told that love, following His example, is our response to who He really is and His love for us. We show His love to each other and Him.

In consultation presentations I used to tell audiences that if God had a business card it would likely say, "I'm God and you're not." It's a truth so easy to state but sometimes difficult to accept, especially when we want to be in charge.

You have likely heard this expression or words like it: "Not fully knowing what is to come creates anxiety and causes fear, no matter how much planning may have occurred, or how many negotiations have been concluded and contracts signed."

Here is great news. Fear is not a part of God's will for us nor is it a method He employs.

God's love is pure and perfect.

> Fear is not a part of God's will for us nor is it a method He employs. God's love is pure and perfect.

And we are told this:

I John 4:16-21 (NIV) (underlining by author)

¹⁶And so we know and rely on the love God has for us. <u>God is love. Whoever lives in love lives in God, and God in them</u>. ¹⁷ This is how love is made complete among us so that we will have confidence on the day of judgment: <u>In this world we are like Jesus</u>. ¹⁸ <u>There is no fear in love. But perfect love drives out fear, because fear has to do with punishment</u>. The one who fears is not made perfect in love. ¹⁹ <u>We love because he first loved us</u>. ²⁰ Whoever claims to love God yet hates a brother or sister is a liar. For whoever does not love their brother and sister, whom they have seen, cannot love God, whom they have not seen. ²¹ And he has given us this command: <u>Anyone who loves God must also love their brother and sister</u>.

A lot is packed into a few sentences. Among the truths we can readily see:

1. Love is a defining characteristic of God and those who follow Him.
2. Love's "completion" gives us confidence when judgment comes because of Christ's provision. The completion part is composed of at least our acceptance of the provision of Jesus, and our willingness to submit to Him fully.
3. We are "like" Jesus when we demonstrate His love for others, even if it costs, and it may.
4. Fear cannot coexist with this kind of love. Worry is erased, too.
5. Perfect love drives out fear.
6. Fear is equated with punishment and a lack of confidence in God. Or stated another way, fear is seen in a lack of faith in Him.
7. We love in response to His love. His love for us came before ours and was given to us because of grace. His love is our model.
8. We are commanded to love each other as Christ loved us and gave Himself for us.
9. One who hates "a brother or sister" and claims to love God at the same time, is lying.
10. We obey His command to love others. Obedience to His command says we want His will, not ours.

Therein is the first part of the Breakthrough. Willingly let God be in charge through faith, and employ His love no matter the circumstances because we are submitting and

Faith Matters

obeying. There is no other way to reach a Breakthrough and there is no fear of the future in this kind of letting go.

This Breakthrough is available to all who submit to God and seek His will. When you and I do these actions, fear is erased and we live in complete confidence that no matter what occurs, God's love will be our gift both to receive from Him and to give away, doing it like Jesus did. That includes loving others even if they are not yet Christ followers.

> Willingly let God be in charge through faith, and employ His love no matter the circumstances because we are submitting and obeying. There is no other way to reach a Breakthrough and there is no fear of the future in this kind of letting go.

Remember, Christ died for us when we were unworthy, showing love to all who had not yet believed. That is one of the reasons that you are more important than what you do, or have done. This relationship is always unmerited and cannot be earned. It is revealed through God's grace and our gracious acceptance of it.

> God's love will be our gift both to receive from Him and to give away, doing it like Jesus did.

Love is never to be hidden or hoarded. What we've received we freely give in gratitude for all He has done.

The Breakthrough of authentic faith, which I am convinced every believer should truly desire, is one that is granted because we choose to live in and through God's love and follow His ways without reservation. We want Him to lead completely, no selfish agendas or hidden motives on our part. This is authentic faith in action.

> Love is never to be hidden or hoarded. What we've received we freely give in gratitude for all He has done.

We openly declare this truth. Because He openly declared it and showed it on a cross in sacrifice, He wants us to actively be willing to do the same. Early Christians and still many today are openly persecuted for their faith. These lives and testimonies speak volumes to all believers about God's provision in all times, including the highly difficult ones.

> We want Him to lead completely, no selfish agendas or hidden motives on our part.
> This is authentic faith in action.

Chapter 9
Share Your Journey

Here is one of my favorite scripture passages, **Matthew 5:15, 16 (NIV):**

> [15] Neither do people light a lamp and put it under a bowl. Instead they put it on its stand, and it gives light to everyone in the house. [16] In the same way, let your light shine before others, that they may see your good deeds and glorify your Father in heaven.

It's vital to share your witness to the Breakthrough of faith you have found or are discovering. Telling your story can encourage others in their quest for God in their lives. If you share, you offer truth and encouragement. Don't hide your light; let it shine.

One of the reasons for establishing Creative Team Publishing (**www.CreativeTeamPublishing.com**) is to do just that. Since 2007 it's been a huge honor to see people's stories come into print!

Responsibilities accompany desires to share a faith story. One is to tell the truth accurately. The other is to make sure that your story points to God's action, not necessarily yours alone, though your viewpoint of your journey has value, certainly.

It's about God's involvement in creating life change in which we have willingly participated. Telling others what God has done for us can shine a light for them to see God's work as possibility and reality in their lives, too. People should see and hear how God has worked in us, as examples, and then as the light bearers, we focus on His involvement in our lives (giving Him praise and honor) as testimony or witness.

Music creation and performance presentations have been methods of sharing I have employed for years. I have observed that sometimes music, vocal and instrumental in combination or alone, can speak volumes more than just the spoken word, although every means is important.

For many organizations I have produced and directed choirs and various musical groups, dating all the way back to high school. During ages fifteen to eighteen, I was blessed to be under the influence of two gifted conductors, one at Grossmont High School in La Mesa, California, and two at Skyline Wesleyan Church in Lemon Grove, California where Rev. Orval Butcher was Pastor, and he, by the way, was a supremely talented tenor singer.

Faith Matters

At Grossmont I was exposed to the choral leadership of **Don Hubler** as a member of the nationally acclaimed **Red Robe Choir**. Mr. Hubler was one of the finest choral and ensemble masters of his time. At Skyline, the music exposure came under the leadership of **Derric Johnson** and **Otis Skillings**, internationally known Christian musicians, writers, composers, arrangers, performers, and producers.

In fact, Otis personally endorsed the *Light of Love* album. His endorsement: "Light of Love is original, young, talented, excited, dedicated; its members are for real. These are qualities that make a group stand out from the others, and the qualities that make wonderful ministers for Jesus Christ. Enjoy Light of Love with me … I am sure you will."

Plus, I was exposed and deeply influenced by one of the premier composers and musical artists of the day, **Andraé Crouch**, who also endorsed the *Light of Love* album. What he said: "These brothers truly minister in the Light of Love. Their songs communicate in a new way the love that people are searching for. I like what their songs say, and I'm proud to call them brothers. Keep shining in Jesus!"

Plus, a nationally well-known gospel quartet's music presented contemporary combinations of styles and harmonies that greatly inspired me. I am speaking of *The Imperials*. Members at that time were bass singer Armond Morales, tenor singer Jim Murray, Roger Wiles, Terry Blackwood, and Joe Moscheo on piano. They were an amazing group. I don't think I've ever enjoyed a combination of male harmonies more.

Largely due to their profound and combined influences, I became hungry to lead choirs and small musical groups, writing and arranging music for them, and performing with them. The result was a tremendous outpouring of new original songs, recordings, and travel for program presentations. I remain grateful for those opportunities and the gifted people with whom I worked. *Light of Love*, to which you already were exposed in this book, was one example of a small traveling group.

In church consultation engagements I was fond of joking about two books I wanted to write "someday." One was called *My Awesome Humility and How I Attained It* which was eventually written and published in 2018. (Please see www.myawesomehumility.com.) Another one was to be titled *How to Acquire a Choir*. Both titles caused chuckles and downright laughter in some cases, raised eyebrows in others.

With exposure through performances and music and book publications, also came profound and ongoing responsibilities to let God's light shine to influence others toward Him, while at the same time being gracious for audience approvals and accolades. It's a delicate balance, to be accomplished with integrity and humility.

Faith Matters

Never was this more the case than when I won an **Emmy®** in 2011 for a commercial production, alongside my recording engineer, **Dan de la Isla**, of **DLI Productions** who also took home an Emmy®. Dan's studio is located in Pacific Beach, California, a community near San Diego. The Emmy® Award-winning commercial for Postal Annex+ Sound of Business TV Campaign was produced by Altair Media & Marketing. Video production is owned by Postal Annex+.

A special thank you to Steve Goble, producer and a great friend, for suggesting that an Emmy® could be won for this spot!
~ (Video File © Annex Brands, Inc.; please see www.glenaubrey.com)

Through several commercial productions including the one that was awarded the Emmy® I found myself laboring alongside unbelievably talented individuals. Working on recording and production projects with immensely gifted people represent unique opportunities to allow God's light to shine on others who see good deeds and through your and my witness, are pointed to God.

When you and I are blessed with opportunities to share our faith through exposures great or small, our desires must be to let God's light shine through us in our ongoing commitment to allow God to rule, reign, and receive glory. This is ever part of the package.

I say all this not out of any sense of arrogance; rather, with sincere gratitude for the opportunities given to me to share His message through song, printed and published books, and more.

Our core motive is the key. See this verse, quoting Jesus at a time when unrest was rife against Him. Note that motive centers on who receives glory and praise for any presentations, great or small:

John 7:18 (NIV):

> Whoever speaks on their own does so to gain personal glory, but he who seeks the glory of the one who sent him is a man of truth; there is nothing false about him.

Open doors to share faith and proclaim His truth, no matter the methods or talents employed, cause us to weigh our motives, what we expect to accomplish. Our response and commitment should be that we do all for *His* glory, *not selfish gain* or the desire to promote ourselves.

Faith Matters

> When you and I are blessed with opportunities to share our faith through exposures great or small, our desires must be to let God's light shine through us in our ongoing commitment to allow God to rule, reign, and receive glory. This is ever part of the package.

Accepting gratitude and praise from a humble heart versus accepting gratitude and praise from selfish arrogance again boils down to identifying a central motive. This truth causes one to ask: "What is my real reason for singing, preaching, publishing, or any other means of sharing faith?" It's a question never far from any engagement.

It is right for believers and committed Christ followers to share journeys of faith and our Breakthrough! The question always will remain, "Why do we do it?"

Chapter 10
Be Thankful as You Accept God's Grace and Proclaim His Truth

Truly thankful people freely exercise humble hearts and giving actions born of gratitude, and borne on grace. These traits permeate and become core-characteristic of their activities in their works for God.

In a life of thanksgiving there is no other option than to plainly see gratitude and giving at work in both receiving and giving. The very act of expressing thanksgiving is one of submission to a giver, and thanking someone demonstrates humility as a receiver. Humbly receiving a thank you from another shows true gratitude and thanksgiving must be accepted with grace and love.

This is true when you and I express thanksgiving to God or say a heartfelt "Thank you" to someone who has contributed to us, along with the act of receiving thanks as well.

There is no room in genuinely thankful expressions for arrogance or feelings of superiority. The two, thanksgiving and arrogant selfishness, simply cannot reside in the same person at the same time.

For acts of thanksgiving to be complete, one must accept thanks as well as express it. Thanksgiving and receiving are parts of the same activity.

> In a life of thanksgiving there is no other option than to plainly see gratitude and giving at work in both receiving and giving. The very act of expressing thanksgiving is one of submission to a giver, and thanking someone demonstrates humility as a receiver. Humbly receiving a thank you from another shows true gratitude and thanksgiving must be accepted with grace and love.

We are commanded to be thankful as believers. When the peace of Christ rules in our hearts, thanksgiving is natural.

In Paul and Timothy's letter to the **Colossians, Chapter 3 and verse 15 (NIV),** we read this:

Let the peace of Christ rule in your hearts, since as members of one body you were called to peace. And be thankful.

When God's peace is within, thanksgiving is natural.

Faith Matters

Paul and his student, Timothy, begin writing this letter to the Colossian church by tying thanksgiving to faith, love, hope, and grace, central elements of community in Christ. These characteristics focus attention on giving to others, receiving grace, as well as being gracious.

From **Colossians 1 (NIV)**:

> 1 Paul, an apostle of Christ Jesus by the will of God, and Timothy our brother,
> 2 To God's holy people in Colossae, the faithful brothers and sisters in Christ: Grace and peace to you from God our Father. 3 We always thank God, the Father of our Lord Jesus Christ, when we pray for you, 4 because we have heard of your faith in Christ Jesus and of the love you have for all God's people— 5 the faith and love that spring from the hope stored up for you in heaven and about which you have already heard in the true message of the gospel 6 that has come to you. In the same way, the gospel is bearing fruit and growing throughout the whole world—just as it has been doing among you since the day you heard it and truly understood God's grace.

With humble hearts we accept God's grace as a gift and proclaim Him as Giver and Lord because of that special relationship. There is no room for hostility, revenge, self-aggrandizement, or other less than gracious attitudes and actions.

We started this book with a true story. Let's finish with another.

I was amazed as I witnessed and unfortunately got caught up in ongoing acts of rancor, seeds of unrest, and blatant disrespect among leadership at a Christian organization for which I worked; it was a large church. This church was one of the biggest and most successful in our city. The staff was highly talented and publicly acclaimed.

However, I, too, as a member of the leadership team, became part of the problem: partly through ignorance and partly intentionally as a defense mechanism. Either way, my activities were just as wrong and misguided as others on the staff.

To those who witnessed our staff's ministry activities from the outside in, the image was one of ministry success. But the inside day-to-day operations were anything but peaceful and contributory. This was not the body of Christ in action. That was the real truth from the inside out. Several ministry participants who were leaders were anything but dedicated to selfless outreach; dedicated, rather, to selfish image building in front of the masses.

At one particularly unsettling meeting of leadership staff, false accusations and blatant lies were told. In a secular organization it could have cause for a lawsuit at worst, or resignations at least. It was generally accepted that whatever occurred during the week, Monday through Saturday had to be endured, as long as "it all came together on Sunday." Authentic faith, simply, was absent.

The differences between Sunday's public appearance and weekday strife were remarkable, and generally unknown to outside observers. What a charade! The word "fake" or "false" described the true staff relationships and contributions away from public view. What a shame.

I concluded that the only degree of consistency present was the inconsistency of the words and activities of leader-participants, many of whom hungered for power, position, and prestige away from public observance and knowledge. "Giving" and "godly" attitudes and actions of love and grace between highly gifted people had been replaced with, or substituted by crippling innuendo, destructive gossip, and overt, and at times covert displays of raw selfishness and power positioning. It became very difficult to work and minister there.

One of the congregants who didn't know what was really occurring was my father. He thought that to work for a church could be a great opportunity. To him, it represented a dream job, the true behind-the-scenes elements of which I believe he never knew. He only knew what was readily observable and experienced on Sundays. I didn't tell him what truly was occurring, not wanting to shake or shatter his faith, admit my complicity, or give him additional burdens to bear.

I often wondered, "How could any supposedly Christian church demonstrate such ungodly acts among leadership and yet portray an image of love and compassion for the world and other believers in front of weekend audiences?" Those negative characteristics finally brought me to the place of resignation. Not too long before I departed, I asked this question of one senior leader, "Are you kind?" To my recollection, he could not and did not answer.

During my time there as part of ministry staff I definitely learned how not to run a church or any organization for that matter, and how not to treat staff. The picture was bleak.

Years passed and ministry opportunities grew immensely for me in a national organization. While not "perfect" by any means, it was refreshing to a point. At least core activities for the most part were not inconsistent with true faith, at least from my perspective. I worked with this ministry organization for ten years.

Then I concluded it was time to embark on my passion for building teams in multiple churches, theater groups, and universities. I instructed church staffs and non-profit organizations in Southern and Central California, Arizona, Colorado, Texas, and Virginia on how to "do" church, enjoying respect, a growing following, and ministry success.

My job was as a consultant, and my goal was to work myself out of a job over the course of a year or so, by training others in core team leadership and programming arts, consisting of building teams in music, media, drama, technical services, support services, stage design/artistic direction, and administration.

All well and good except for one nagging memory: the large church where I had served in the beginning still had its central leader with whom my relationship had been the most soured and negative. I was training many but had unresolved conflict present within. The memory of the unsettledness "plagued" me and I felt a huge urge to go visit the main leader and try to make things right. It was a leading of God, for sure.

Here's how I know this. My wife and I made the appointment. We went to see him and I sincerely apologized and asked for his forgiveness for things I had said and done that were not contributory, positive, or good.

He not only graciously accepted my apology; he then told me that he felt the same, and asked me to forgive him. It was a heartfelt, touching moment. I forgave him as he had forgiven me.

Quite suddenly the haunting and plaguing memory was erased and a sweet and peaceful relationship was restored. I was so grateful and amazed at God's power at work in that moment of willful submission to Him, following His command to "love one another."

I asked him, "Pastor, how's your health?" He said he was fine, and that he was planning a ministry trip soon. There was joyful anticipation in his voice.

Several days after our in-person meeting, he was dining with his wife at a local restaurant on a Sunday afternoon. Quite suddenly he experienced a brain aneurism and in a matter of moments, he died. The news was heartbreaking. I will never forget his funeral and the gratitude I felt for having been able to "make things right" just days before.

One item of truth emerged after the funeral. Several former staff who had served with me or at a time close to my term of service had actually experienced the same kind of relationship restitution as I had, but that fact was unknown to any of us at the time. Truly amazing, that before his life came to an end, many relationships had been restored!

For me, I began to teach organizational staffs with whom I was consulting far more than just the "tools of the trade." Now I added this message: if there were unresolved conflicts present, it was incumbent on each person to make them right.

This was true partly because none of us knew what the future held, but more importantly because humbly forgiving and requesting forgiveness, owning responsibility and following Jesus' commands to love one another were right actions, good, uplifting, and pure. Simply put, these acts of restoration were the right things to do.

Actions of deep contriteness and genuine humility were then and are now central requirements of learning and following God's will. Humbled attitudes opened doors of understanding, promoted God's peace, and became preparatory to learning and following His commands fully, experiencing a deepening, authentic faith, a true Breakthrough.

As was stated before:

> We see authentic faith at work in people's lives who are fully submitted to God, His promises, and purposes.
> That is the Breakthrough!
> Authentic faith is evidenced in principle and practice.

Closing Thoughts

When this book's writing was about fifty percent completed, excitedly I contacted my friend who in January of 2019 had wished us both a Breakthrough for the New Year. I told her about the central truths you have read. She shared my enthusiasm and agreed fully. We had discovered the true Breakthrough.

I wish for you the same result.

The Breakthrough for us may take many forms, both intangible and perhaps tangible. Regardless, if we are persons of faith and desire to know and serve God better, fully humbling ourselves and submitting willingly to following His Word and commands, we will experience a Breakthrough of God-birthed dimensions. It is spiritual, yes, and will impact every area of our lives if we allow—in fact, the Breakthrough in relation with God is the transformation of our entire way of living, our entire selves, by Him. It is not merely a set of principles to follow: no, it is an entirely new way of living.

It will also serve to light the paths of many others with whom we have contact. Share the journey with those around us and give glory to God. There is no better option. Be encouraged in these quests to know Him more and the truths He offers to you and me. Our lives will be richly transformed.

In 2007, I was recording a piano album of heritage hymns, or older songs of the church. I wanted to record **There Is a Redeemer,** thinking the song was not under copyright any longer, rather, in the public domain. However, I discovered the song was not nearly as old as I originally thought, and was still under copyright. One problem: the album's cover art with that title was already completed.

How to solve this dilemma? Well, I concluded the best way would be to write and produce a brand new song with the same title. So that's exactly what occurred. Here are the words followed by a simple piano score.

I don't think any other song I've written expresses my true sentiments more. It's here for you to enjoy.

There Is a Redeemer

Lyrics and Music by Glen Aubrey © 2007
All Rights Reserved.

Lyrics:

There is a Redeemer, Jehovah, Who saves us.
Forgiven, we bow down to worship our Lord.
Amazing compassion that seeks those who wander
And brings them to His light, redeemed and restored.

His love is forever and reaches to lost ones
To buy back the souls who will turn and believe,
Who stand in His presence, forgiven completely.
Unworthy, yet fully accepted, received.

We sing, "Alleluia," give glory and honor
To Jesus, the Savior, Who rules everything.
No other shall sever this love bond, and never
Shall we cease to praise Him, our God and our King.

Music:

Recommended Reading

It would be impossible to list all the resources written to defend the truth of history, and it is not the intention of this author to thus engage. Personal study has been sufficient for me, and I encourage you to investigate matters of belief and faith because faith matters.

For example, Google this: Who has tried to disprove the Resurrection and come away as a believer? Among the 844,000 results as of 2019:

- *Evidence that Demands a Verdict* by Josh McDowell
- *More Evidence that Demands a Verdict* by Josh McDowell
- *An Atheist Investigates Jesus to Disprove the Resurrection* by Lee Strobel
  https://www.focusonthefamily.com/parenting/spiritual-growth-for-kids/an-atheist-investigates-jesus-to-disprove-the-resurrection
- *The Case for Christ* by Lee Strobel
- *Cold-Case Investigator Turns to Science to Disprove Christ's Resurrection, Gets Shocked by the Evidence,* 04-01-2018, Paul Strand

Recommended Reading

And these publications deal with the Bible as truth, especially the Gospels, and explore whether these writings are reliable to your faith. Among 3,460,000 resources:

- *Mere Christianity* by C. S. Lewis
- *The Word Became Flesh* by E. Stanley Jones
- https://www.josh.org/history-prove-gospels/
- https://zondervanacademic.com/blog/who-wrote-gospels
- https://en.wikipedia.org/wiki/Historical_reliability_of_the_Gospels
- https://www.beliefnet.com/faiths/christianity/do-we-have-proof-that-the-gospels-are-true.aspx
- https://www.history.com/news/was-jesus-real-historical-evidence
- https://www1.cbn.com/there-archaeological-evidence-support-gospels
- http://evidenceforchristianity.org/evidence-for-the-reliability-of-the-gospels/
- https://carm.org/what-gospel-q-and-does-it-prove-gospels-are-false
- https://www.christianity.com/jesus/is-jesus-god/the-gospels/how-do-we-prove-the-gospels-are-inspired-by-god.html
- https://www.startingwithgod.com/knowing-god/what-is-faith/

May your investigation and study be an inspiration to you and others who want to discover truth.

Credits in Order of Appearance

The King James Version of the *Holy Bible* (KJV), Public Domain.

New International Version (NIV) *Holy Bible*, New International Version ®, NIV® Copyright ©1973, 1978, 1984, 2011 by Biblica, Inc. ® Used by permission. All rights reserved worldwide.

Freedom Light, Expressions of Hope and Evidence
ISBN 9780979735875
© 2009 by Glen Aubrey.
All Rights Reserved.

Core Teams Work ... Their Principles and Practices
ISBN 9780979735806
© 2007 by Glen Aubrey. All Rights Reserved.
Revised Edition © 2019 by Glen Aubrey.
All Rights Reserved.

E. Stanley Jones:
The Word Became Flesh, Library of Congress Catalog Card Number 63-9936, © 1963 by Abingdon Press. All rights in this book are reserved.

Credits In Order of Appearance

If God Be For Us, original song by Glen Aubrey, Recorded by *Light of Love,* 1974, © 1974 by Glen Aubrey and © 2019 by Glen Aubrey. All Rights Reserved.

Abraham Lincoln quote:
https://www.brainyquote.com/quotes/abraham_lincoln_388944

Light of Love, music group, 1974.

The Leadership Trilogy for Business Core Team Development:
    Books published by Creative Team Publishing
        www.CreativeTeamPublishing.com

1. *Leadership Is ... How to Build Your Legacy*
   ISBN 9780983891987 © 2005, 2012 by Glen Aubrey. All Rights Reserved.
2. *Industrial Strength Solutions ... Build Successful Work Teams!*
   ISBN 9780985597931 © 2005, 2012 by Glen Aubrey. All Rights Reserved.
3. *Core Teams Work ... Their Principles and Practices*
   ISBN 9780979735806 © 2007, Revised Edition © 2019 by Glen Aubrey. All Rights Reserved.

The Core Team: A Functioning Workable Solution (Table) from *Industrial Strength Solutions.*

Credits In Order of Appearance

Robert F. Dees, Major General, U.S. Army, Retired: Author published by **Creative Team Publishing**.
https://resiliencegodstyle.com

His Love for Us: original song by Glen Aubrey, © 1977 by Lillenas Publishing Company and reassigned to Glen Aubrey in 1984; Music and Lyrics © 2019 by Glen Aubrey. All Rights Reserved.

As an Example: original song by Glen Aubrey, Music and Lyrics © 1973 and 2019 by Glen Aubrey. All Rights Reserved.

Harvey Tellinghuisen: music transcription for *As an Example*

Grossmont High School, La Mesa, California: Don Hubler, choral conductor, Red Robe Choir.

Skyline Wesleyan Church, Lemon Grove, California: Derric Johnson and Otis Skillings, music directors and internationally known Christian musicians, writers, composers, arrangers, performers, and producers.

Andraé Crouch: internationally known Christian artist and song writer.

The Imperials: nationally known gospel quartet.

Credits In Order of Appearance

Emmy® 2011: Award for a commercial production for **Postal Annex+ Sound of Business TV Campaign, produced by Altair Media & Marketing and Postal Annex+.**
Video File © Annex Brands, Inc.

There Is a Redeemer: original song by Glen Aubrey, Music and Lyrics © 2007. All Rights reserved.

Products and Services

Books authored by Glen Aubrey referenced in *Faith Matters* are listed and described at this website:
www.CreativeTeamPublishing.com

Order through:
Amazon.com
barnesandnoble.com
indiebound.org/

Titles:

Freedom Light
ISBN 9780979735875

<u>Leadership Trilogy for Business Core Team Development</u>

1. *Leadership Is ... How to Build Your Legacy*
   ISBN 9780983891987
2. *Industrial Strength Solutions ... Build Successful Work Teams!*
   ISBN 9780985597931
3. *Core Teams Work ... Their Principles and Practices*
   ISBN 9780979735806

My Awesome Humility and How I Attained It
ISBN 9780997951950

The Author

I enjoy traveling, especially to Gettysburg, Washington, D.C., Europe, and the Middle East. I treasure multi-cultural experiences and am fulfilled when conducting conference center presentations and speaking engagements. Enjoyments in life include walking, bicycle riding, and being with family and close friends; also a fireplace, my dogs, listening to classical music and profound artistic works. I appreciate, compose, and arrange multiple styles of music. I earnestly engage in creatively stimulating conversations on uplifting topics, listening and responding to other people's well-thought-out perspectives. I love to laugh. I thoroughly enjoy good football and baseball games. I am a student and teacher, a follower and leader.

Further, "I acknowledge that I have a long way to go in learning what life is all about. I acknowledge that I am willing to work hard to achieve what I believe I am called to do. I also willingly and joyfully acknowledge dependence on God."

~ From *Lincoln – The Making of a Leader* by Glen Aubrey © 2017

The Publisher

Creative Team Publishing (CTP)

If you are an author: "We Want to Publish Your Creation!"
www.CreativeTeamPublishing.com

You are invited to contact Glen Aubrey for products and services.

www.glenaubrey.com

www.ingramcontent.com/pod-product-compliance
Lightning Source LLC
Chambersburg PA
CBHW030440010526
44118CB00011B/730